Enchanted Island

Crissa Constantine

© Copyright 2013, Crissa Constantine

All Rights Reserved.

No part of this book may be reproduced, stored in a retrieval system, or transmitted by any means, electronic, mechanical, photocopying, recording, or otherwise, without written permission from the author.

ISBN: 978-1-625-17192-4

Parksville Beach

The Parksville Community Beach, where the Sandcastle Days are held every summer, is delightful all year. Kids of all ages walk their dogs, fly kites, stroll on the boardwalk, jump around in the playground, and walk for hours on the beautifully sandy beach that stretches out forever when the tide is out. The ocean is too shallow for a harbor here, making it a perfect place to relax.

Crissa Constantine

Solo Piano

Crissa Constantine

Parksville Beach

Crissa Constantine

Copyright © 2011 Crissa Constantine

Enchanted Island

Enchanted Island

Crissa Constantine

Enchanted Island

Seagulls and Herring

It is a fantastic experience to watch hundreds of frenzied seagulls swarming high in the sky above the ocean as they hunt during the March herring season on the East Coast of Vancouver Island.

Solo Piano

Crissa Constantine

Seagulls and Herring

Crissa Constantine

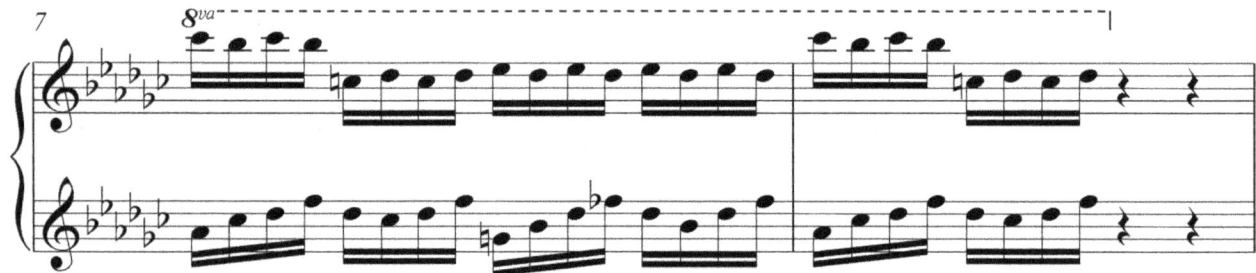

Copyright © 2011 Crissa Constantine

Enchanted Island

Crissa Constantine

Enchanted Island

Crissa Constantine

Enchanted Island

19

Crissa Constantine

Enchanted Island

Enchanted Island

Crissa Constantine

24

Enchanted Island

Fog-Sun

The Oceanside area of east Vancouver Island can be choked with fog in the fall, but when the sun disperses it, everything comes back to light and life and dances with joy.

Solo Piano

Fog-Sun

Crissa Constantine

Andante, Misterioso

Enchanted Island

29

Crissa Constantine

Allegro

Enchanted Island

Crissa Constantine

Allegro Moderato Maestoso

Enchanted Island

Crissa Constantine

Enchanted Island

Crissa Constantine

Enchanted Island

Crissa Constantine

Enchanted Island

Qualicum Beach

The ocean is mainly calm and dreamy here, but it sometimes erupts into huge foamy waves that smash onto the beach with tremendous force, spraying pebbles and seaweed onto higher ground. The Island mountain chain makes a fantastic backdrop.

Solo Piano

Qualicum Beach

Crissa Constantine

Andante

Enchanted Island

Crissa Constantine

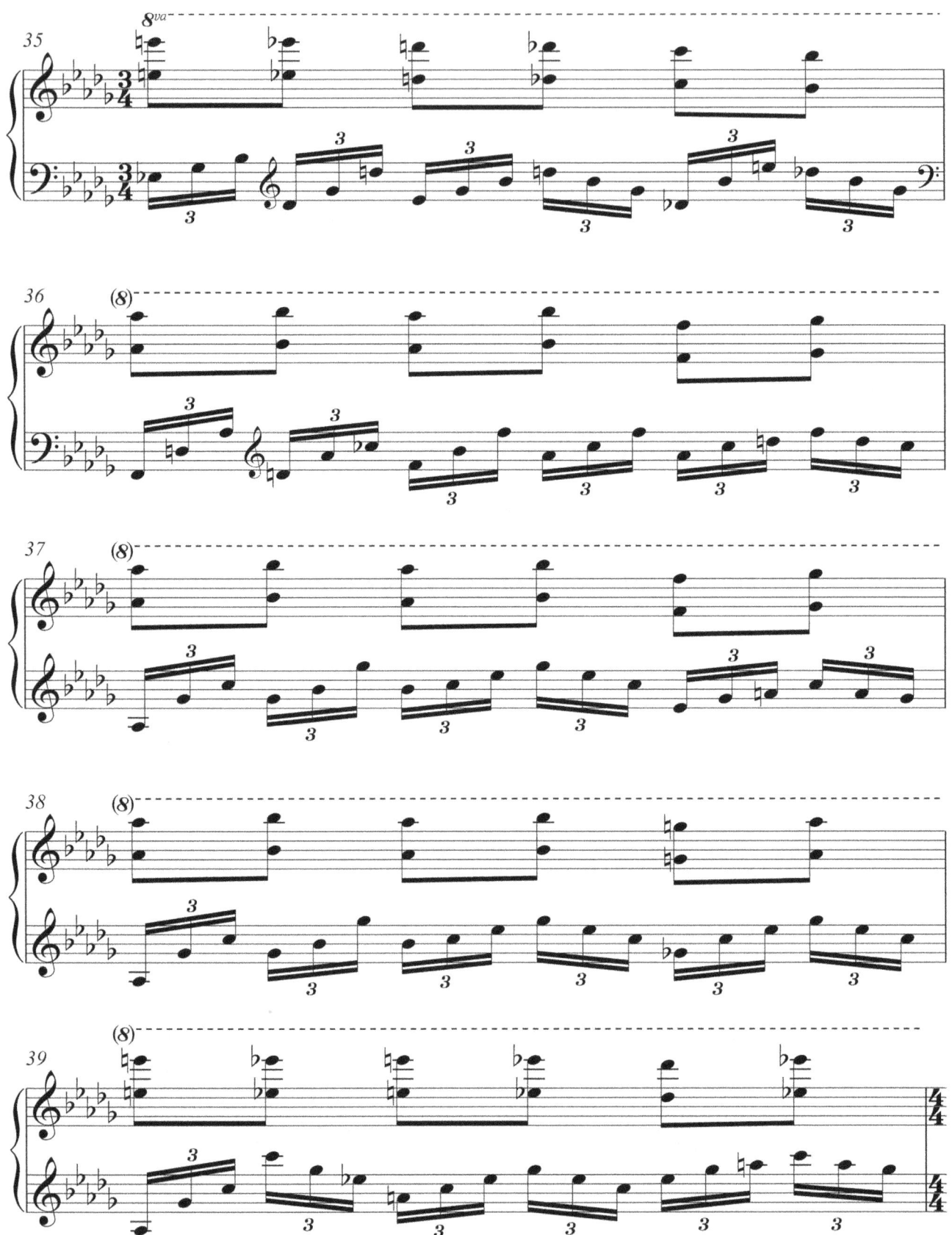

Enchanted Island

45

Crissa Constantine

Crissa Constantine

Enchanted Island

Maestoso

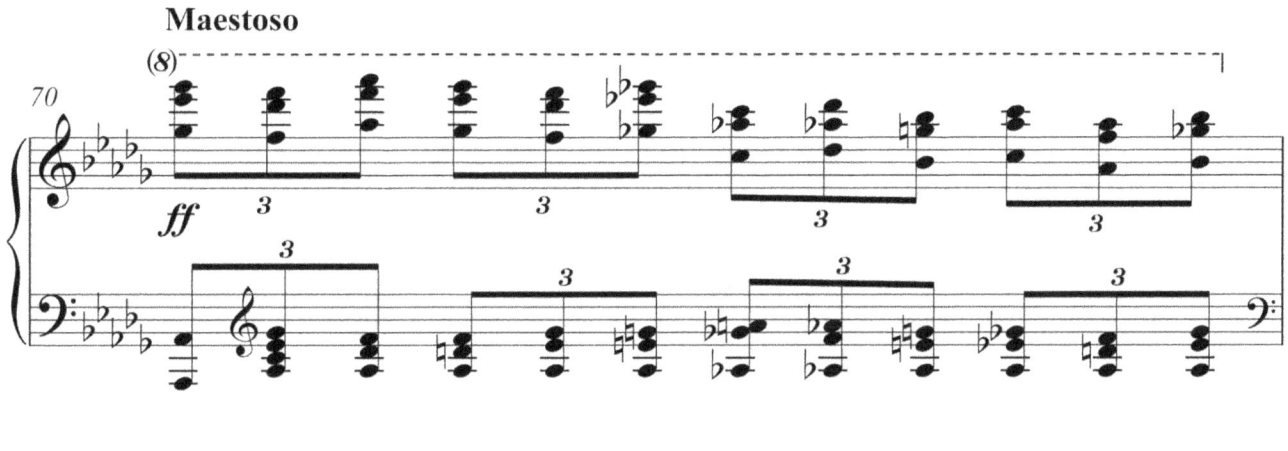

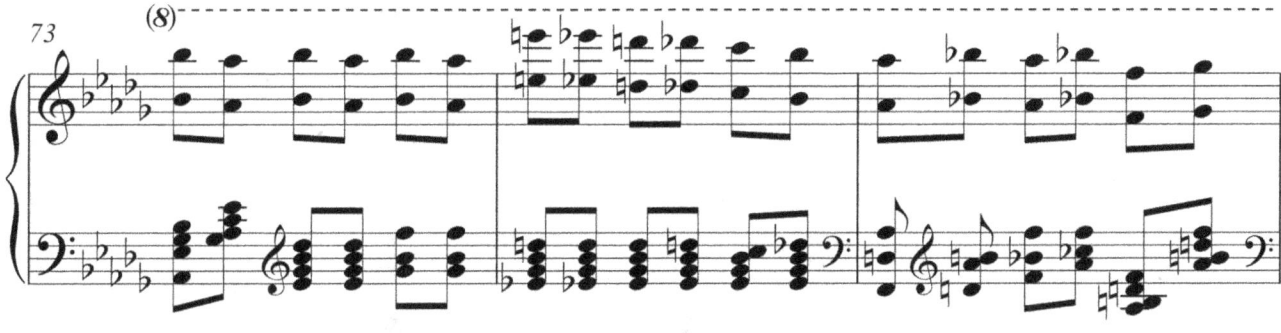

49

Crissa Constantine

Enchanted Island

51

Crissa Constantine

Enchanted Island

Crissa Constantine

Enchanted Island

Rathtrevor Beach

One can walk for hours on this incredibly sandy, shallow beach just south of Parksville. Its panoramic beauty caresses and warms one's soul, with the sound of the gentle waves reaching into the nearby forest. When wild roses bloom, the whole park is pink and redolent with perfume.

Solo Piano

Rathtrevor Beach

Crissa Constantine

Moderato

Enchanted Island

Crissa Constantine

Enchanted Island

61

Crissa Constantine

Enchanted Island

Crissa Constantine

Enchanted Island

Crissa Constantine

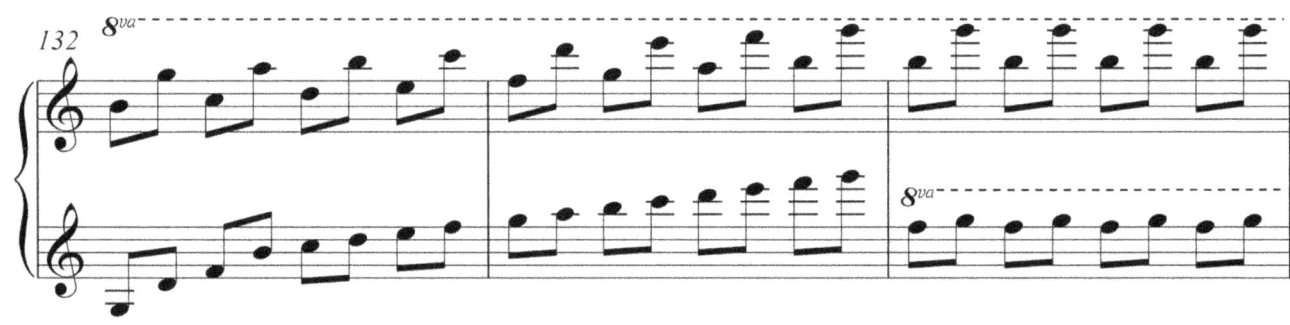

Long Beach

It is a profoundly spiritual experience to stand on the shores of Long Beach on the west coast of Vancouver Island and watch as the endless powerful waves smash against rocky islets, sending gigantic plumes of ocean spray high into the air.

Solo Piano

Long Beach

Crissa Constantine

Enchanted Island

71

Crissa Constantine

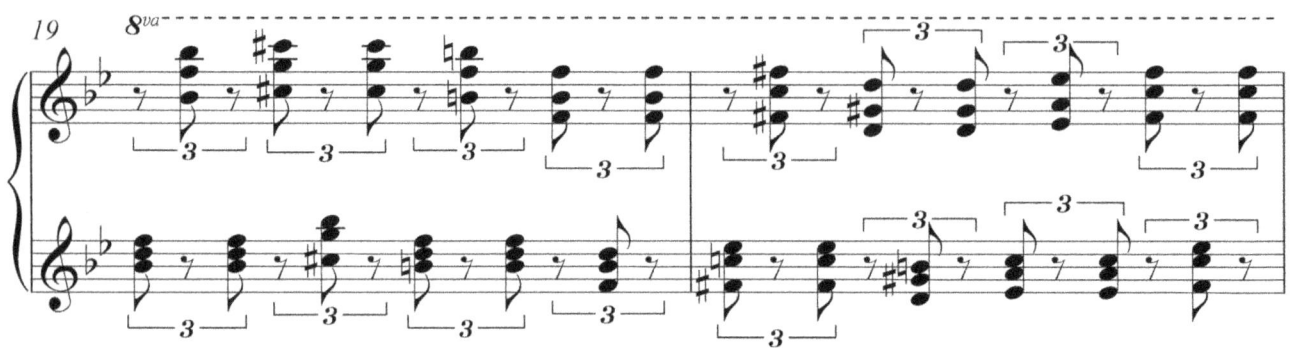

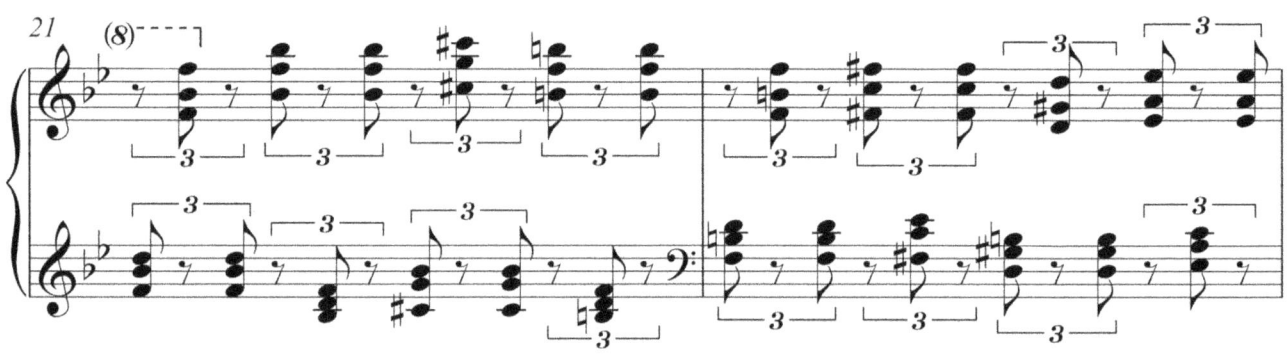

Enchanted Island

Crissa Constantine

Enchanted Island

Enchanted Island

Crissa Constantine

Englishman River Falls

One truly lives in the "now" when standing under the tall trees and watching the roaring, frothy water crash over the rocks toward the emerald river far below the cliffs.

Solo Piano

Englishman River Falls

Crissa Constantine

Copyright © 2011 Crissa Constantine

Enchanted Island

Crissa Constantine

Enchanted Island

Crissa Constantine

Enchanted Island

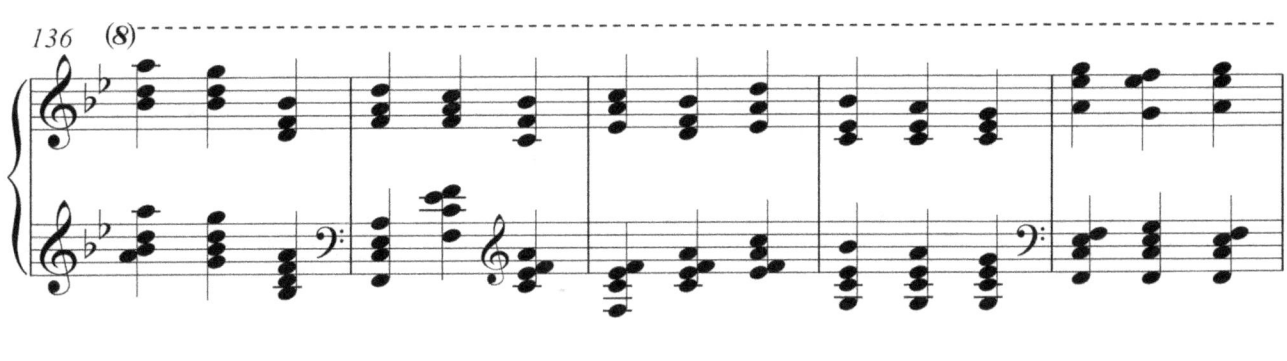

Crissa Constantine

Saltspring Island

I was dazzled by summer sunlight dancing on the gentle ocean waves as I stood on the deck of the small ferry from Crofton to Saltspring Island. The island is a magically happy place.

Solo Piano

Saltspring Island

Crissa Constantine

Enchanted Island

Crissa Constantine

Enchanted Island

Crissa Constantine

Enchanted Island

Crissa Constantine

Allegro giocoso